HANDS-ON LATIN AMERICA

ART ACTIVITIES FOR ALL AGES

ART FROM THE ANDES

As long ago as 1500 B.C., the Chavin, in northern Peru, created pottery covered with animal figures...especially cats. The Paracas, 3,000 years ago, wove brilliantly patterned fabrics and wrapped their dead in the yardage. The Chimu crafted goldwork that was prized by their Inca, then Spanish, conquerors. The colorful aryballo jar has stored fermented drinks for centuries. The woven dolls, alpaca clothing and wall hangings, incised gourds and crafted baskets are traditional ancient patterns but recent purchases. The art that has flourished for centuries continues today with few changes in pattern and color.